OPTIONS TRADING

A Step-By-Step Guide for Investing in the Stock Market and Improve Your Trading Skills. How to Set Up A Great Source of Passive Income and Establish Financial Freedom

Written by **David Johnson**

The Options Trading Checklist

(<u>Good Luck</u> Trading Without this...)

This checklist includes:

- ❑ 5 Option Strategies that Every Trader Should Know About!
- ❑ 5 Stocks to Buy in the 2020 Stock Market Crash
- ❑ The Top 3 Options Trading Strategies for Beginners
- ❑ The 5 Secrets of Getting Rich (Bonus)

To receive your survival checklist, visit the link below:

https://davidjohnson.activehosted.com/f/9

Furthermore, the information that can be found within the pages described forthwith shall be considered both accurate and truthful when it comes to the recounting of facts. As such, any use, correct or incorrect, of the provided information will render the Publisher free of responsibility as to the actions taken outside of their direct purview. Regardless, there are zero scenarios where the original author or the Publisher can be deemed liable in any fashion for any damages or hardships that may result from any of the information discussed herein.

Additionally, the information in the following pages is intended only for informational purposes and should thus be thought of as universal. As befitting its nature, it is presented without assurance regarding its prolonged validity or interim quality.

Table of Contents

Introduction

If you have spent any time looking at the world of investing, you may have heard about options. They are sometimes going to seem pretty overwhelming to think about, but if you know a few key points that come with them, options can be pretty easy to understand. Options are another class of assets, just like mutual funds, ETFs, bonds, and stocks. And when the investor properly uses them, they can offer you some unique advantages that trading with the other assets just can't. You can purchase options like most other asset classes, by using an investment account from a brokerage. Do a bit of research with these ahead of time to ensure you find the right brokerage firm for your needs. Options can be a powerful tool because they will do some wonders with enhancing your portfolio.

Options can provide you with this advantage as they offer a source of additional income, greater protection, and further leverage. Based on the situation, you will find some options contract that can provide you with an adequate alternative. In turbulent times, options are a great means of protecting your portfolio against sharp and unexpected declines.

Besides protecting some of your personal assets, options are sometimes used to generate a recurring income. And some investors will choose to use these in a more speculative purpose, such as wagering on the direction that a stock will take. Just like with any of the other choices that you make with investing, options will involve some risks, and you must understand these and know how to avoid them as much as possible. Therefore, any time you want to trade options with a broker, there will be some kind of disclaimer like the following to help you know about the risk with options: Options involve risks and are not suitable for everyone. Options trading can be speculative in nature and carry a substantial risk of loss. Only invest in risk capital. Options are going to belong to a larger group of securities that are known as derivatives. This is a word that many investors are going to associate with excessive risk-taking. In the past, Warren Buffett has even referred to these derivatives as a weapon of mass destruction for the stock market.

While there is some truth to this assertion, with the irresponsible use of derivatives, the fact is that most derivatives are a good way for smaller investors to make some tidy profits. However, it is important to know that a derivative is a financial instrument that is based on the value on what is known as an "underlying asset." This means that the valuation of the contract will depend on the valuation of the asset it is tied to. It should also be noted that you never own the asset when you take out an option until that option is exercised. By the same token, you never actually sell the asset until the option goes through.

Now, there are going to be an impressive deal of different securities that fall under this kind of label, including calls, swaps, forwards, futures, and puts. If you already know how these options are going to work, and the right way to use them, you will have an enormous advantage when trading in the market. Options are also nice because they will ensure they put the odds in your favor. If using options as speculation doesn't seem to fit with the risks you want to take or your trading choices, then you can also do options with no speculating. Even if you decide to never work with options, it is important to understand how companies you invest in will use them. Some companies may use this to hedge their foreign exchange risk or give employees some stock ownership. And most of the multi-national corporations today will work with options in some form or another, and even as an individual investor, you can use it to invest in many securities.

There are two main types of options. We call the first a "call option." This option receives this name as it gives the bearer the right to buy. However, it does not make up an obligation. What this means is that, if for whatever reason, the bearer chooses not to exercise their option, they do not penalize this. If the contract is exercised, then the bearer must go through with the purchase of the underlying security at the price agreed. We refer this price to as the "strike price."

The second option is called a "put option." This option means that the bearer may sell the underlying asset, but the contract itself does not represent an obligation to go through with the deal. This means that if the seller changes their mind, they are free to do so as long as the provisions in the contract are met.

One way that you can think about a call option is like having a down payment for a future purpose. For instance, a potential homeowner sees that in an area of their town, there is a recent development that is about to go up. This homeowner may decide that they want the right to purchase one home in that area in the future, but they only want to exercise that right once there are certain developments built around that area. Maybe they want to make sure that they build there some schools first or some other great amenities before they purchase. These kinds of circumstances could then affect the decision of the homeowner to purchase the home in that area. The potential homebuyer would enjoy the option of buying or not depending on whether the promised amenities show up, and they can agree to purchase the home at a predetermined level.

In this example, the potential buyer could benefit if prices for that property, or that sector, go up. Let's assume that both the seller and buyer agree at a sale price of $100,000. The buyer gets a call option for this price for a period of two months. At the maturity of the option, the buy may purchase the property. In addition, the seller cannot sell the home to anyone else during that period, even if the market value of the property goes up, and other buyers offer more money. The seller can negotiate but cannot make a deal unless the option is exercised or declined.

If, after the two-month period, the option is exercised, the buyer goes through with the deal paying the $100,000 strike price. The buyer can make an impressive deal of money if the valuation of the property increases. For instance, if the valuation goes up to $125,000, the buyer can then turn around and resell at a higher price. The option also protects the buyer in case the price of the property falls. For instance, if the valuation falls from $100,000 to $80,000, the buyer has the option to decline. This can save the buyer from losing on the deal. The seller misses out on the sale and would have to figure out what to do with the property moving forward.

Therefore, options are seen as insurance policies. They can protect investors from purchasing assets which may suddenly decline in value, or lock in the price of an asset which is expected to go up at some point. If the buyer, or seller, decide not to go through with the option, they only lose the underwriting fee that goes along with the option itself.

Chapter 1

Options Trading Basics You NEED to Know About

What is an Option?

You probably know what a stock/share of a company is - in the simplest of terms, a single share represents a solitary unit of ownership of a company.

Companies offer their shares for sale to raise capital for themselves, and such shares (also referred to as equities) are listed and traded in a stock exchange.

In a stock exchange, many high-profile shares that trade in enormous volumes may also have derivatives associated with them. A derivative is a contract between two or more parties in which the contract 'derives' its value from underlying security such as a stock or an index.

The most-traded derivatives in the stock market are Futures and Options. They are also referred to as F&O.

Futures contracts are relatively easier to understand when compared to options, but they carry more risk and are less flexible.

An option is defined as a type of contract, sold by one party to another that gives the buyer of the option, the right, but not the obligation, to buy or to sell the underlying stock at a pre-determined price.

Options cannot exist indefinitely, and every option has an expiry date. The option buyer of a specific option may have a right to exercise his/her option only at the time of expiry of the option, or he/she may have a right to exercise the option at any point in time till the date of expiry.

Types of Options

Here are two different distinct types of options. They are:

1. Call Options – These options give the buyer the right to buy the underlying security at a fixed price.

2. Put Options – These options provide the buyer the right to sell the underlying security at a fixed price.

The most important thing to know here is that with a call option, the buyer of the option can only start profiting from that option when the value of the underlying stock/index goes up.

In the case of a put option, the buyer of the option can only start profiting when the value of the underlying stock/index goes down.

European Style and American Style Expiries

There are two different conventions that are followed globally by exercising an option.

1. European Style Expiry - Call options and put options following the European style expiry are denoted by CE and PE. In this style of expiry, we can exercise options only at the specified time of expiry.

2. American Style Expiry - Call options and put options following the American style expiry are denoted by CA and PA. In this style of expiry, we can exercise options at any time until the specified time of expiry.

The options traded in any stock exchange will follow either of these two conventions, depending on the norm in the country. For example, all options traded in India's NSE follow the European style of expiry.

Basic Terms used in Options Trading

Before getting into examples, here are explanations of the most basic terms one needs to know before getting into options trading.

1. The Strike-Price (SP)

All options contract will have an associated strike-price. This is the fixed reference price against which settlement takes place at the time the option is exercised or when the option expires. For any stock/index that is traded in the Futures and Options segment, there will be different options contracts corresponding to various strike-prices. These strike-prices are pre-determined by the stock exchange in which that underlying stock is traded.

For example, the stock of Infosys - the Indian IT giant, that is traded on India's NSE, has a market price of ₹1030 and has an entire range of associated put and call options available with strike-prices such as 960, 980, 1000, 1020, 1040.

With call options, the strike-price effectively functions as the 'buy price' while the market price of the underlying stock functions as the 'sell price' at the time of settlement or exercising of the options.

With put options, the strike-price effectively functions as the 'sell price' while the market price of the underlying stock functions as the 'buy price' at the time of settlement or exercising of the options.

2. The Lot Size

The lot size specifies the fixed number of units of the underlying security that one options contract covers. The lot size is determined by the regulatory body within the stock exchange and might vary from stock to stock.

For example, the current lot size for the Indian IT company Infosys, which is traded on the Indian NSE, is 500. So, any trader, who buys 1 option of Infosys (irrespective of the type, strike-price or the expiry date), holds buy/sell rights on 500 shares of Infosys. If you buy 1 Infosys call option with a strike price of 1020, it means your contract gives you the power to buy 500 shares of Infosys at strike-price of 1020., if you buy 1 Infosys put option with the strike price of 1000, your contract gives you the right to sell 500 shares of Infosys at 1000. Since the lot size is fixed at 500, you cannot have an option to control only, say, for example, 200 shares or 150 shares through an option–you will always buy/sell in multiples of 500 only.

The market lot sizes for stocks traded in F&O are revised by the stock exchange from time to time.

Note: In the US NYSE, they standardize the lot size at 100—in other words, a single options contract entitles the buyer of the options to 100 shares of the underlying stock/index.

3. The Premium

The premium is the amount of money an option buyer pays per share when buying an option (or the amount of money an option seller receives per share for selling an option).

The premium of an option at any point in time depends on using various parameters (often referred to as the Options Greeks—something we will cover later on).

The total cost of any options contract, therefore, will be the premium multiplied by the lot size for that underlying. For example: If the premium of an Infosys call option with strike-price 1040 is₹5, then the cost of that options contract is₹5 x 500 (lot size) =₹2,500.

4. The Expiry Date

Every single option has an expiry date.

Expiry of options traded in any exchange could happen on a weekly, monthly, or even quarterly basis. These dates of expiry follow a rigid calendar determined by the exchange in which they trade the options.

For example: the options for the Bank Nifty (an index of Bank stocks), traded on the Indian NSE, have a weekly expiry and any Bank Nifty option slated for expiry in a given week will always expire on the Thursday of that week., All monthly options traded on the Indian NSE, slated for expiry in a given month, expire on the last Thursday of that month.

At any point in time, there could be multiple monthly contracts available for a given stock depending on the exchange in which that stock is traded.

For example, Stock options for any stock trading on the NSE are available for 3 consecutive trading months at any point in time. So, if you are in the month of March 2017 (any day before the last Thursday), you could trade monthly options for the months of March 2017, April 2017, and May 2017, and all these options expire on the last Thursday of their corresponding month. When the options for March 2017 expire, they will make the options for June available for trading in the NSE, and so on and so forth.

Why should anybody trade in Options?

These are the 4 main reasons why Options Trading is an attractive proposition for those who are keenly interested in the equity markets.

1. Options Limit Risk

The biggest advantage of buying an option is that your risk is limited to the amount of money you pay as premium.

Think of Bob's Call option trade.

When Bob thought there was a chance of cow prices going up, he paid money upfront and entered a contract with Jacob to sell him 5 cows at $2,000 each; Bob did not actually buy the cows upfront.

Instead, if Bob had bought 5 cows straightaway from Jacob by paying the entire cost of cows at $10,000 (this is synonymous with regular stock trading where one takes delivery of the stocks bought) and if the price of cows had fallen by $500 instead of going up by $500, he would have lost $2,500. By entering an option contract, Bob stood to lose a maximum amount of only $250, if cow prices were to fall.

So that was a smart move, wasn't it? That's how an options contract can limit risk.

2. Options Provide better Leverage for Money

Options provide excellent leveraging power, and a trader can buy an option position that imitates a stock position almost identically but at an enormous cost saving.

Let's go back to Bob's trade.

What would have happened if Bob spotted the opportunity for a profitable trade but had only $1,000 to spare to buy cows and did not know about options?

He could not have even bought a single cow for that money and would have lost the opportunity to earn a sizeable profit.

But when Bob bought an options contract instead of buying the actual underlying asset, the dynamics of the trade changed.

The entire investment for Bob in his trade was a paltry $250! The premium he paid was only the fraction of the total cost of 5 cows for which he bought the rights to sell. He practically controlled assets worth $10,000 ($2,000 x 5) by that contract he bought for $250.

This is one of the most fantastic advantages of options trading—better leverage for money!

3. Options can provide a higher percentage of returns

An options trader has to pay only a fraction of the asset's value to control the actual asset. This gives the trader a chance to earn much more than what could be earned by purchasing that asset upfront and then selling it.

Let's break this down.

In Bob's trading example, the market price of a cow at the beginning of the trade was $2,000.

If a regular cattle trader, with no knowledge about options trading (unlike our astute Bob), had $2,000 in hand and believed the price of a cow could go up, he would have been able to buy just one cow from Jacob and would have made just a profit of $500 when the price of cows went up—a profit of 25% given that his investment was $2,000.

On the other hand, if Bob had $2,000, he might have probably used $2,000 to buy 8 options contracts at the premium of $50 that gave him purchasing rights for 40 cows instead.

And given the $500 appreciation for the price of each cow that followed, Bob's profit would have been $18,000 ($500 profit per cow x 40 minus $2,000, the total cost price of the contracts) with an investment of just $2,000.
That's a ridiculously high 900% return for the same amount of money!

4. Options help in hedging Futures or Intraday trades

Many traders often buy or short-sell Futures contracts expecting one particular directional movement or the other. Intraday traders also do something similar – they buy/short-sell a large batch of shares in expectation of either an up move or a down move in the day's course.

If such traders get their directional call wrong, they could end up facing huge losses because, in either case, unless a stop-loss (a point at which you cut losses and get out) is started, the potential for profit or loss is more or less unlimited.

No trader will complain about unlimited profits when trading Futures or when trading stocks using intraday margins. But if you were to engage in Futures trading or intraday trading without hedging your positions, whenever you encounter losses, it could go to the extent of wiping out your entire capital and perhaps far more. In essence, you could actually end with debts more significant than what your overall capital in Futures and intraday trades were because you would have been trading using margins (3-4 times the leverage on your existing capital) given by your broker.

If you know how to trade options, you can buy a call or put options to ensure your trade against unlimited loss–the moment your futures/intraday positions turn against your expectations, the options will cover your loss.

Note: Technically speaking, unlimited losses can take place only with positions that are shorted (short-sold) because there is no upper limit for the price of any share. However, for a long position, the losses incurred will hit the ceiling once the price of the share reaches 0.00 (while on paper, this is a limit to losses, huge drops in any share associated with a Futures trade would be enormous enough to wreak financial havoc for a trader).

Chapter 2

5 Golden Tips You MUST Know Before Starting Trading

Golden tip #1: Understand what options are

As a wise investor, you will equip yourself with the information on the investment that you engage in. Knowing is very important. It gets even better if you have the right information. Before embarking on an options trading investment journey, first know what it entails. Studying will help you identify if it is an investment that you find worthy of spending your income on or not. All this is aimed at making the process easier for you.

As more and more people become familiar with options trading, we are having an increase in the number of people engaging in the trade. The problem, however, is that we are having an extensive amount of people incurring losses in options trading. This situation results from the fact that people engage in options with very little knowledge of what it entails and end up regretting making terrible choices. To avoid such mistakes, conduct proper research that will guide you into making the right investments.

Golden tip #2: Do not assume that it is a simple thing to do

With the continued increase in awareness of options trading, we have a lot of beginners think it is an elementary thing to do. Well, if you approach options trading with this misguided belief, you are likely to make mistakes. These errors will cost you and make you end up making a loss. If you have been an investor for long enough, by now, you must have realized that any significant investment that results in maximum profits is never dull. If at all that was the case, we would never have people making considerable losses in options trading.

When you familiarize yourself with information regarding options trading, you will discover that there are a lot of complicated terms. You will need to take some time and learn most of the terms and there meaning. You can compare options trading to building a house. The core determinant of having a stable structure is the foundation that you layout. While trading options, you will need to have a firm foundation for you to become an expert in trading. It will demand that you exercise some patience and trust that eventually, you will become a skilled investor. The trick is never to assume that investment is simple or easy but to consider each with a lot of importance. This helps you to stay focused and to avoid making unnecessary mistakes while carrying out a trade.

Golden tip #3: Invest what you can afford

As a beginner in options trading, you may be looking for an investment where you intend to invest all your finances. With various traders giving success stories on how they earned millions from trading, you may think of it as a worthy investment that will cause you to spend all of your finances in the trade. You may end up experiencing a loss and lose all that you invested in. Before engaging in options trading, you must treat it like any other investment. Do not spend all your emotions in it. Investments at times lead to excellent outcomes, but they can also result in a loss. For this reason, the only part with that which you can afford to lose.

Do not let the desire to get rich quickly overwhelm you and make you think it comes easy. You don't just buy options and immediately start earning from them. There are some factors that you will have to consider. Look at the option types, the pricing, the strategy, expiry date, and the convenience depending on the situation at hand. Not all that glitters is gold. You will find that if you use a strategy that was used by a friend, it may fail to work. They could have earned good returns, but you end up with losses.

Golden tip #4: Risk management

Options trading has its own risk. Depending on the type of option you intend to engage in, it is good to navigate through the possible expected risks. By knowing the risks, you can come up with ways of managing them so you can avoid or prevent getting losses. As an investor, you will realize that, at times, investments will push you to the edge and so you will need to come up with ways in which you can handle such situations.

Sometimes, you may have to choose between making no profit and incurring a complete loss. The probability of earning an income from a particular opportunity may be low, and hence, they would be no need to bet on the slight possibility of getting returns. As a wise investor, you can decide that you would instead earn no profit and prevent incurring a total loss. For you to even realize some of these things, it will require that you evaluate the direction of stocks to know how to manage the risks.

Golden tip #5: Evaluation of the option strategies

There are many ways to kill a rat. This also applies in options trading; there are many ways to carry out a trade. Depending on the type of options you trade, different strategies can favor some. I have explained the various options, strategies, and illustrated how each one of them works. You will find that the way they carry a particular option to trade out may vary from the other type of option. We see this difference in both put and call options.

Some strategies are simpler than others, and hence, they may appear to be more appealing since you can comprehend easily. The problem, however, is that they may not always work. The option strategy that led to a successful trade today may result in an unsuccessful business. You are more advantaged if you manage to know all the viable strategies you can use. That way, you can use a fresh approach if another strategy cannot give you the desired results. Never get used to one policy, learn to change depending on the situation at hand. This will prevent you from losses.

Bonus Tip 1: Be timely

The time factor is a core necessity in almost all investments that you will ever engage in. You find at there is a specific time the stakes are likely to give you high returns, and there are times the investments will acquire a low return. The only differentiating factor is timing. As an investor, it is good to establish when to trade and when not to engage in a trade. You can make this decision by evaluating the stock market. Look at the times when the returns are high and utilize them. Consider the period when yields are low and avoid investing in such times.

Time is also vital in determining the validity of options. Options have a duration up to which they are valid. An expiration date determines if an option can be traded, and when it reaches a trade cannot be carried out. After expiration, a contract can be regarded as worthless, so it no longer has value. As an investor, you will be required to be keen on the expiration date to avoid making your contract useless. Putting this factor into consideration will enable you to minimize losses and maximize profits.

Bonus tip 2: Look at the profitability

While investing in options, consider the liquidity of the option. Some investments will reap good fruits, and others will result in a total loss. As you analyze the various investments that you can engage in, you must assess the possible returns that they can generate. You would choose to participate in more profitable investments. After all, you are in business to make profits and create a sustainable income at the end of your investment.

The options are priced differently depending on the type. You will find that some options will demand that you invest a lot, but the chances of high profitability are very high. Others have low profitability, and they require minimal investments. If you are looking into generating a considerable income, you can choose to invest in the more profitable option. This way, you will be sure of high returns. Does this mean that you cannot spend it if you have a low income? Well, no, you could still have little, but you manage to invest in that which you can afford. The returns may be small, but at least you will have improved your past earnings.

Bonus tip 3: Evaluating the technical analysis

Familiarize yourself with that options trading structure. Asides from knowing what it entails, go the extra mile to understand how it works. Be keen while evaluating the charts and graphs. Search for consistent patterns. Know why options move in specific directions and understand how that affects your trade. Know the investments that can result in a successful outcome and those that cannot and those that may result in a complete loss. You will make the right decisions if you put this into consideration.

This analysis can also guide you in choosing the right market strategy. Having an excellent plan influences the income that you generate from an investment. Some policies will provide a high possibility of getting a profitable venture, while others will result in a loss. Therefore, you should be keen while deciding on which option strategy to use depending on the situation at hand. With options, if you cannot make money, you will end up losing money quicker than expected. Before engaging in any trade, it is good to conduct a technical analysis to know your chances of earning.

Chapter 3

Options Basics

According to the rules governing options trading, whoever takes a purchase option on a house has not yet bought that house but has the option (the right) to buy the house within a certain period. In the financial markets, they pay an amount for an option to the person granting the right (the so-called option premium).

You cannot buy without a seller, so there are always two parties involved. The profit of one is, therefore, losing another, we call this a 'zero-sum game.' However, both the buyer and the seller can both earn money if the seller holds shares to cover the options. The profit on the shares then compensates for losing his option.

Call and Put

Call: A call has a right to an underlying buy at a convincing price within a certain period.

Sell: a sell is a right to an underlying asset to sell at a specific price within a certain period.

If you have a right, you can exercise it. If you have a duty, you are in a dependent position, and you have to wait for the counterparty to exercise its right. To acquire the privilege of the underlying, the buyer has to pay a premium to the seller (writer). Remember, before entering a duty, you want a consideration, a payment, or a premium in money. Options are a standardized product, so everyone can trade them at the same time on equal terms. For example, the same specifications apply to your neighbor with the same option as you (although the costs per broker can differ).

Options can be applied both defensively and offensively, depending on the objective of an investor. A defensive investor will use options differently than an offensive trader. It is precisely that aspect that makes options a product that deserves a place in every investment portfolio. There are also many options because of the combination of options, which you only have with options and not with shares, but we will deal with that later. Options are the best invention after the wheel. Just like with a wheel, you can also roll options to a later expiry date, but more about that later. First, realize that during the entire term, you can either buy or sell options during the whole term. So, you don't have to wait until the last trading day.

Buy and Sell Call Options

The big difference between buying or selling options is that you buy a premium when you buy options, and you receive a premium when you write, so there is a risk that the counterparty, so the buyer, can exercise his option if the expiration option has value.

Long call (Buy a Call)

You can compare buying a call option with an option on a house: you may (but do not have to) buy a house for, for example, € 350,000 within a certain period. Suppose the house increases in value to € 400,000, you can exercise your purchase right, and you have a profit of € 50,000. In options trading, unlike a house, an option is not free, but the buyer must pay the price (the option premium) to the agent of the option. Notice how the graph line increases up the theoretical P/L axis as basic aid increases in price, illustrating that this position benefits from an increase in the price of the basic aid.

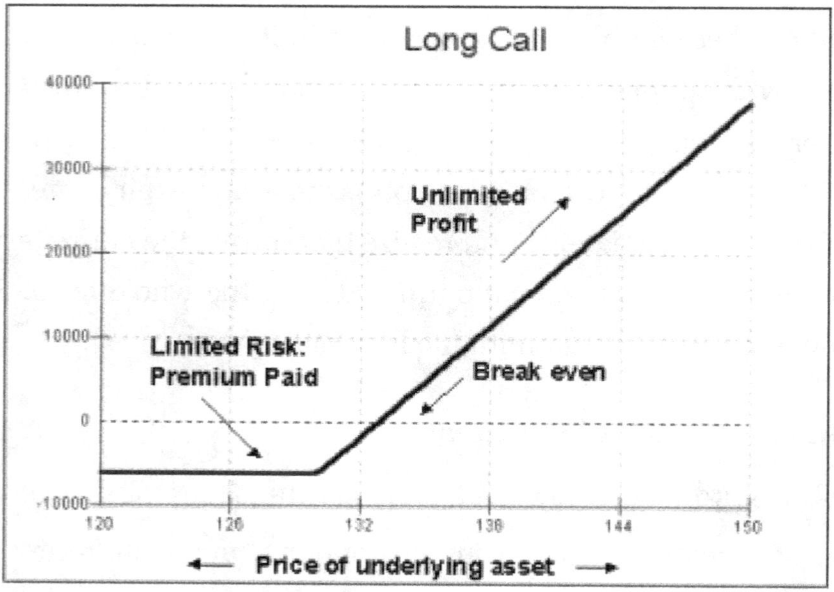

The graph above shows a call option on option ABC with an exercise price of $10 for which $1 has been paid. The more the share rises, the higher the premium of the call and, therefore, the profit. The break-even rate (the price where neither profit nor loss is made) is $10 + 41 = $11. Loss is limited to the determined option premium of $1. This is times 100 because the option relates to the elemental amount of 100 shares, so here it is $1 x 100. Even if the stock drops to $0.01, you can never lose more than the paid option premium of $100. Imagine the option quotes $15.88. The call is, therefore, at least worth $5.88 because the net asset value is 15.88-10 = $5.88. The profit, in this case, is $ (5.88-1) = $4.88: a profit of 488%.

Short call (Sell a Call)

The seller of a call option has an obligation (but not the right) to deliver a fixed amount of an underlying asset at a predetermined price, the exercise price. Sellers calling an option can best be compared with an insurer who speculates on the do not pass a certain event: an underlying rise above a certain price. In the short call position chart, it shows the limited reward as the position graph line levels out just above the break-even line. It shows the risk increasing to an unlimited amount as the underlying asset price increases.

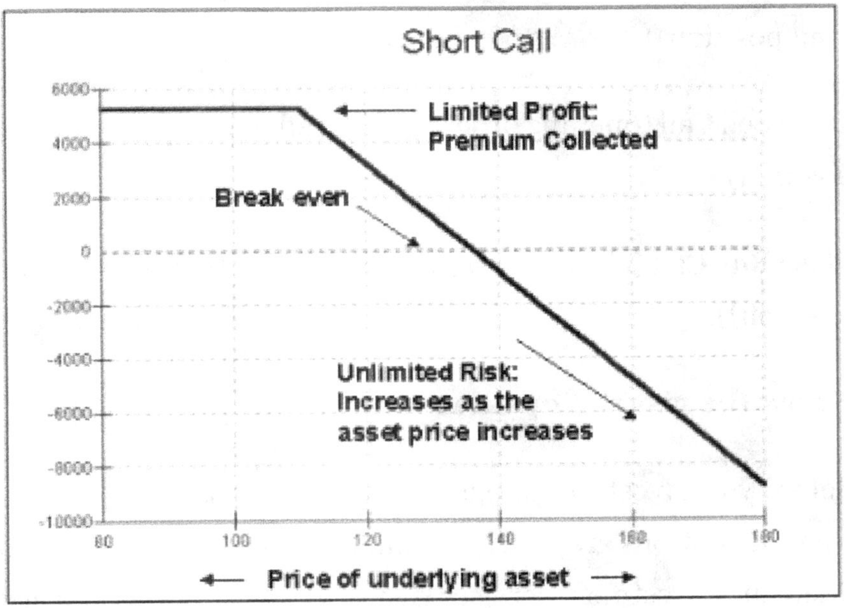

The graph of a short call (see figure above) is, therefore, the reverse of the long call of the example mentioned above. The profit is limited to the $1 received. The selling call option diminishes as soon as the option exceeds $11. The loss at a rate of $13 then amounts to $2 (x 100), which is $200 on expiration. Although the option is worth $3, the premium received $1, which can be deducted from this.

When trading in call options, there are the following order options:

Open Buy Call (opening order of a purchased call option (opening long position)).

Close Sell Call (closing order of a purchased call option (closing long position)).

Open Sell Call (opening order of a sell call option (opening short position)).

Close Buy Call (closing order of a sell call option (closing short position)).

Know the risks of options

Before you invest in options, it is essential that you first learn what the options are, but more importantly, what the risks are. There are investment services that work with options and claim that you need not know about options, but that you have to follow their advice. We think it is better that you know what you are doing. If the entrepreneurs had bought those interest rate derivatives on the advice of their bank, they would have done so, because then they would not have suffered substantial losses. In the following article, we will discuss the differences between purchased wells and sold wells.

Purchasing and Vending Put Options

I explained everything about the difference between buying and writing call options. In this part, I will discuss the difference between buying and writing put options. The client of the option put has the right (but not the obligation) to a fixed quantity of the underlying asset to sell at a predetermined price and within a specified period. In a long put, the graph line increases the theoretical P/L axis as the underlying asset market price decreases. This illustrates that this position benefits from a decrease in the price of the underlying asset.

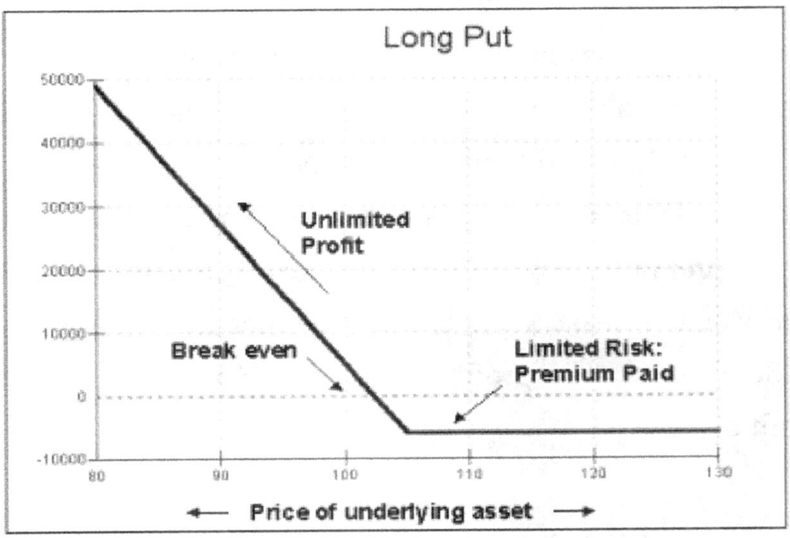

Long put (Buy a Put)

You can compare a put with an insurance policy for a house: you can ensure your house for, for example, $350,000 within a certain period. Suppose your house drops in value to $300,000, you can exercise your sales right and you have a profit of $50,000. In the option trade, an option is not free, but the buyer of this insurance must pay the price (the option premium). The special thing about this insurance through options is that it is unnecessary to have the underlying asset, but you can purchase the insurance separately. Compare it with that you want to ensure someone else's house against a fall in value.

The graph above shows a put displayed on the ABC option with an exercise price of €10 they have paid for which €1. The lower the share goes, the higher the premium of the put and, therefore, the profit. The break-even rate in this case is $10- $1 = $9. It limits the loss to the paid option premium of $1. This is times 100 because the option relates to the underlying value of 100 ABC options, so here it is $1x 100. Even if the price of the option rises to $50, you can never lose more than the paid option premium of $100 if ABC quotes $5.88. The long put is then worth at least $4.12 because the net asset value is $10 - $5.88 = $4.12. The profit is therefore ($4.12- $1) = $3.12: a profit of 312%.

Short Put (Sell a Put)

The seller (writer) of a put has a responsibility (but not the right) to purchase (buy) a set amount of an underlying asset at a predetermined price, the exercise price. In the short put Position Chart, the limited reward is shown leveling out. It shows the risk increasing to an unlimited amount as the underlying asset price decreases.

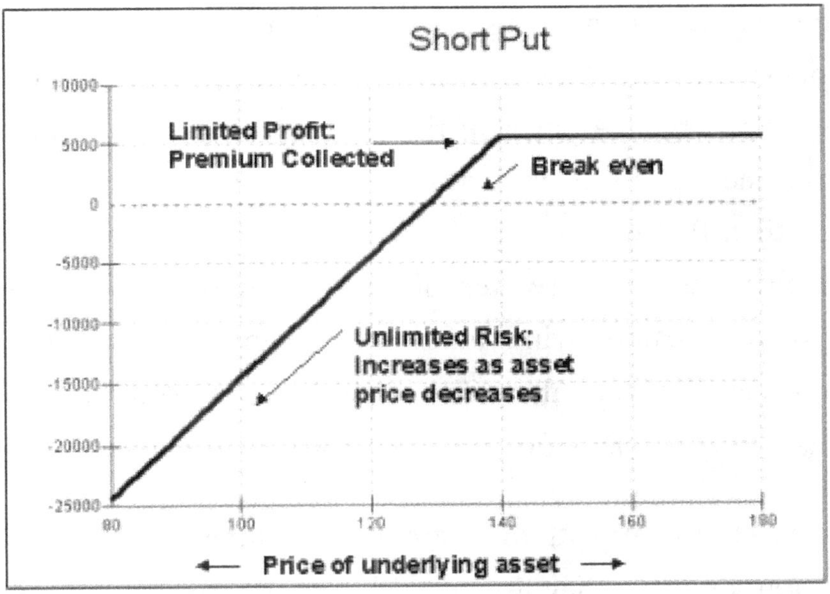

You usually first have to own something to sell it, but with options, it is not. For most people, this is weird and requires an alternative way of thinking to understand how that works. How can you sell something that you don't have, or go short? This is possible with options, but there is something in return: an obligation to supply or purchase Realize that this is not the same as buying a call. To better understand this, you can again use the fire insurance example, but now you are the other side, so the insurer. You offer insurance, and you now receive a premium from the person who takes out the insurance with you, but there is a consideration in return! You can write/sell an option, and you will receive money for it.

You can compare sellers of put options with an insurer speculating on the non- occurrence of a certain event: an underlying value that does not fall below a certain price. The counterparty (the buyer of the put) pays a premium for this insurance to the seller (writer). You don't get that money just like that, that would be a bit too good. There are certain risks involved. As a seller (writer) of a put, you have an obligation to purchase the underlying value if it falls below the exercise price. Your bank/broker will not just allow you to take on these risks; this is only possible if you have a sufficient margin (deposit).

Let us clarify this with the example of a selling put option on an option. Suppose they list these shares at $10. The put option that gives you the obligation to buy these shares in 6 months at 10 dollars now yields $1 per share. The counterparty has the right to sell the shares, but you have an obligation to purchase these shares at $10 if the buyer of the put so wishes. To sell the option securely, you must already set aside enough money in your account to meet your obligation in 6 months. You need $10 (minus the premium received of $1) per share if the buyer exercises this option. You need to take a few risks with this money because you must always remember you must purchase these shares at $10. For each sold option, that is, 100 ABC shares, If the price drops to $7.50 you will suffer a loss of ($2.50 - $1) for every sold put, so that means $1.50 times 100 as you can see in the graph above. You can also choose to close the option early, so you no longer have the purchase obligation. Another possibility is to roll the written put option to another expiration date.

Chapter 4

Brokers

For selecting brokers, you have many options available. There are full service, discount, online, etc. Understanding the differences between them and selecting the ones best suited for your purposes is crucial if you wish to succeed. Another area that a lot of beginners ignore and then receive a rude lesson in is the regulations surrounding options trading.

There aren't too many rules to comply with, but they have significant consequences for your capital and risk strategies.

Choosing a Broker

Generally, there are two major varieties of brokers: Discount and full service. In fact, a lot of full-service brokers have discount arms these days so that you will see some overlap. Full service refers to an organization where brokerage is just a part of a larger financial supermarket.

The broker might offer you other investment solutions, estate planning strategies, and so on. They'll also have an in-house research wing, which will send you reports to help you trade better. Besides this, they'll also have phone support in case you have questions or wish to place an order.

Once you develop a good relationship with them, a full-service broker will become a good organization to network. Every broker loves a profitable customer since it helps with marketing. A full-service broker will have good relationships in the industry, and if you have specific needs, they can put you in touch with the right people.

The price of all this service is you paying higher commissions than average. It is up to you to see whether this is a good price for you to pay. You need not sign up with a full-service broker to trade successfully. Order matching is done electronically, so it's not as if a person on the floor can get you a better price these days. Therefore, a full-service house will not give you better execution.

Discount brokers, on the other hand, are all about focus. They help you trade, and that is it. They will not advise, at least not intentionally, from a business perspective, and phone ordering is nonexistent. That doesn't mean they reduce customer service. Far from it.

Commissions will be lower as well, far lower than what you can expect to pay at a full-service house. The downside of a discount brokerage is that you will not receive any particular product recommendations or solutions outside of your speculative activities. Many people prefer to trade (using a separate account) with the broker they have their retirement accounts with; they keep so everything in-house.

So, which one should you choose? Well, if you aim to keep costs as low as possible, then select a discount broker. In fact, only where you're keen on keeping things in one place should you choose a full-service broker. These days, there's no difference between the two options otherwise.

An exception here is if you have a sizeable amount of capital, worth of half a million dollars. In such cases, a full-service broker will be cheaper because of their volume-based commission offers. You'll pay the same rate or as close to what a discount broker would charge you, and you get all the additional services. Whatever additional amounts you need to invest can be handled by the firm through their wealth management line of business.

There are a few terms you must understand, no matter which broker you choose, so let's look at these now.

Margin

Margin refers to the number of assets you currently hold in your account. Your assets are cash and positions. As the market value of your positions fluctuates, so does the amount of margin you have. Margin is an important concept to grasp since it is at the core of your risk management discipline.

When you open an account with your broker, you will have a choice to make. You can open either a cash or margin account. To trade options, open a margin account. Briefly, a cash account does not include leverage within it, so all you can trade are stocks. There are no account minimums for a cash account, and even if they are, they're minuscule.

A margin account, on the other hand, is subject to weird rules. First, the minimum balances for a margin account are higher. Most brokers will impose a $10,000 minimum, and some will even increase this amount based on your trading style. The account minimum achieves nothing by itself, but it acts as a commitment of sorts for the broker.

The thinking is that with this much money on the line, the person trading will be more serious about it and won't blow it away. If only it worked like that. Anyway, the minimum balance is a hard and fast rule. Another rule you should know is the Pattern Day Trader (PDT) designation.

PDT is a rule that comes directly from the SEC. We classify anyone who executes four or more orders within five days as a PDT ("Pattern Day Trader," 2019). Once this tag is slapped onto you, your broker will ask you to post at least $25,000 in the margin as a minimum balance. Again, this minimum balance does nothing, but the SEC figures that if you screw up, this gives you enough of a buffer.

Each strategy by itself plays out over a month or more, so once you enter, all you need to do is monitor it, and you can adjust it. However, if you will avoid the PDT, you're limited to entering just three positions per workweek.

My advice is to study the strategies and to start slowly. Trade only one instrument at first and see how it goes and then expand once you gain more confidence. At that point, you'll have enough experience to figure out how much capital you need. Remember that even exiting a position is considered a trade, so PDT doesn't refer just to trade entry.

Margin Call

One other aspect of margin you must understand is the margin call. This is a dreaded message for most traders, including institutional ones. The purpose of all risk management is to keep you as far away as possible from this ever happening to you. A margin call is issued when you have inadequate funds in your account to cover its requirements.

Remember that your margin is the combination of the cash you hold plus the value of your positions. If you have $1000 in cash, but your position is currently in a loss of -$900, you'll receive a margin call to post more cash to cover the potential loss you're headed for. In fact, you'll receive it well in advance. If you don't post more margin, your broker has the right to close out your positions and recover whatever cash they can to stop their risk limits from being triggered.

The threshold beyond which your broker will issue a margin call is called the maintenance margin. Usually, you need to maintain 25% of your initial position value (that is when you enter a position) as cash in your account. Most brokers have a handy indicator that tells you how close you are to the limit.

The leading cause of margin calls is leverage. With a margin account, you can borrow money from your broker and use that to boost your returns. Let's look at an example: if you trade with $10,000 of your own money and borrow $20,000 from your broker to enter a position, you control $30,000 worth of the position. Let's say this position makes a gain of $10,000 to bring its total value to $40,000.

You've just made a 100% return on this investment (since you invested only $10,000) despite the total return on the position is 33% (10,000/30,000). What happens if you lose $10,000 on the position, though? Well, you just lost 100% despite the position losing only 33%. Leverage is a double-edged sword.

It is far too simplistic to call leverage bad or good. It is what it is. If you're a beginner, you should not be borrowing money to trade under any circumstances. When you're experienced, you can do so as much as you want. Please note, I'm differentiating between the leverage where you borrow money, and the leverage options provide.

With options, a single contract gives you control over a larger pie of stock, but the option premium still needs to be paid. It is, therefore, cheaper to trade options than the common stock. If you were to borrow money to pay for the option premium, then you're indulging in foolish behavior, and you need to step away.

There's a difference between leverage being inherent within the structure of the instrument and using leverage to increase the amount of something you can buy. The latter when you're a beginner.

Execution

A favorite pastime of unsuccessful traders is to complain about execution. Their losses are always the broker's fault, and if it weren't for the greedy brokers, they'd be rolling in the dough, diving in and out of it like Scrooge McDuck. Complaining about your execution will get you nothing. A big reason for these complaints is that most beginner traders don't realize that the price they see on the screen is not the same as what is being traded on the exchange.

We live in an era of high-frequency trading, and the markets' smallest measurement of time has gone from second to microseconds. Trades are constantly pouring in, and the matching engine is always finding suitable sellers for buyers. Given the pace of the market, it is important to understand that it is impossible to figure out the exact price of an instrument.

Therefore, within your risk management plan, you must make allowance for times of high volatility when the fluctuations will be bigger. For now, I want you to understand that just because the price you received differed from what was on screen doesn't mean the broker is incompetent.

How do you identify an incompetent broker? Customer service and the quality of the trading terminal they give you access to are the best indicators. Your broker is not in the game to trade against you or fleece you. Admittedly, this is not the case with FX, but we're not discussing FX in this book. So, stop blaming your broker and look at your systems instead, assuming the broker passes basic due diligence.

For placing orders with your broker, you have many options. There are different order types you can place, and each order has a specific purpose. First off, we have the market order. This is the simplest order to understand. When you place a market order, you're telling your broker to fill your entire order at whatever price they can find on the market.

A market order results in fast fills unless there's a volatility event of some sort going on. The next type of order you can place is the limit order. The limit prioritizes order price over quantity. For example, if you want to enter 100 units of an instrument at $10, your broker will buy as much as possible under or equal to $10. If they can get just 90 units under $10, then that's it.

A limit order works for a lot of traders looking to enter a position. Directional risk management depends a lot on the size of the position, so it is critical not to exceed the positions limit. For such traders, this is a beneficial order. The last type of order you will encounter is the stop order. The stop prioritizes quantity over price.

Stop orders have a trigger attached to them, and once market price hits the trigger, the entire quantity of the order is executed, irrespective of what the price is. Stop orders are very useful to get out of positions quickly. The stop-loss order is a stop order with the 'loss' in the name referring to the minimization of losses in case the trade goes south.

Another order you should know is the Good till Cancelled or GTC. A cousin of the GTC is the Day order. These two do not order types as much as expiry conditions for the order. A GTC is valid until the trader explicitly cancels it while the day order cancels itself at the end of the market session.

There are over a hundred different types of order your average broker offers you. Do not get bogged down trying to figure them all out. Institutional traders use most of them for specific strategies. To trade well, you need not understand a single word of what those orders are about. Stick to the ones mentioned here, and you can trade successfully.

The question now is, how and where should you use these orders? Well, since you're trading options, you will not be too concerned with stop losses, and your exits will involve letting options expire. Thus, the biggest concern you should have is regarding trade entry.

With options, you can choose either market or limit orders to enter. Personally, I favor market orders since it guarantees you an entry. Risk management here is a bit different from directional trades, so you can afford to enter the market. The only exception is if there are extreme volatility conditions present.

Price Quotes

A lot of traders are stumped when they first look at their trading screens and see that there are two prices for everything. After all, every financial channel always displays one price for security, but when trading, you'll be quoted two different prices within the price box. This is a small but crucial detail for you to understand.

The lower price you receive is called the bid, and this is the price you will pay if you sell the instrument. The higher price is the ask, and this is what you will pay to buy the instrument. The single price you see on your TV screen is the "Last Traded Price" or LTP. Do not make the mistake of thinking the LTP is the actual price since the market moves constantly.

In fact, even the spread (the difference between the ask and the bid) doesn't accurately reflect the genuine state of things thanks to constant movement. There's no need to be alarmed though, as long as volatility is stable, the difference isn't much. Just remember to look at the spread to understand what you'll be paying. The spread increases and contracts constantly, but if you see that it is getting too big, this is a sign that too much volatility exists, and you're better off staying out.

Chapter 5

Top 3 Options Trading Strategies for Beginners

Strategy 1: Strangles and Straddles

This strategy is used when the stock is expected to make a large pricing move, but you don't know the direction that the stock will move. It involves buying a call and put option together in a single trade. A strangle consists in setting a bounding range for the expected stock movement, using different strike prices for the put and call option. A lower strike price is used for the put option, while a higher strike price is used for the call option.

Breakeven price is the breakeven price for the call option if the stock rises, or the breakeven price for the put option if the stock drops.

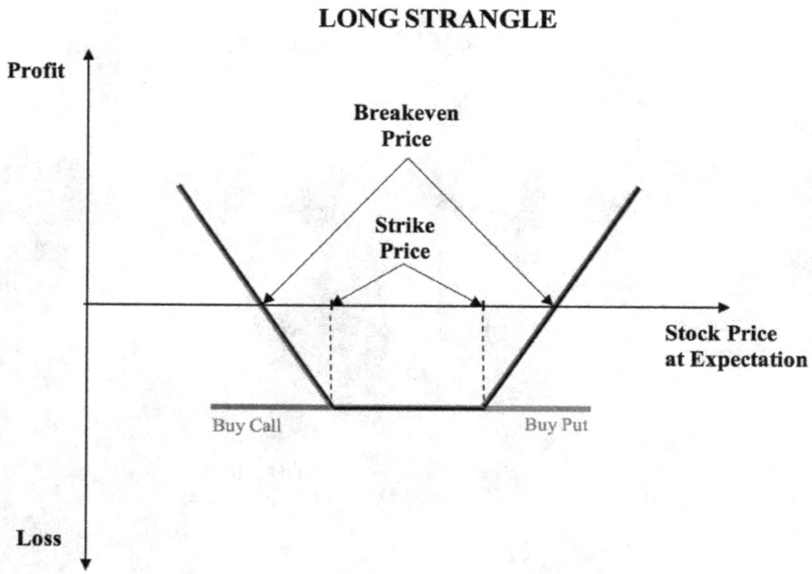

As an example, if the share price of a stock was $100, but it was expected to make a big move, you could set up a strangle with a $105 call option and a $95 put option. If the stock prices cannot move either above the call option strike price or below the put option strike price, you will lose money on the trade. The maximum potential loss is the cost of buying the options.

The strategy is considered neutral because it will make profits if the stock moves up (strongly) or down (strongly). You will invest in this type of strategy when you expect a large move in the stock, so, for example, many traders buy strangles prior to an earnings call. Most earnings calls result in big price movements of the stock, but before the call you aren't sure which direction it will move.

The strike prices selected for the call and put option will be out of the money. Both options will have the same expiration date.

The maximum profit on the upside is theoretically unlimited, but it will depend on how far the stock price moves above the strike of the call option. If that happens, the put option expires worthless, and your profit selling the call option less the cost of buying the put option is your net profit. If the stock price drops, the maximum profit will occur in the unlikely case that it dropped to zero, less the cost of the call option. If the stock price moves to any level below the breakeven price of the put option, you can earn a profit.

We use a straddle for the same purpose, but in this case, we set the strike prices of the call and put option to the same value, and both options will have the same expiration date. With a straddle, you want the stock price to move off the strike price used in either direction.

LONG STRADDLE

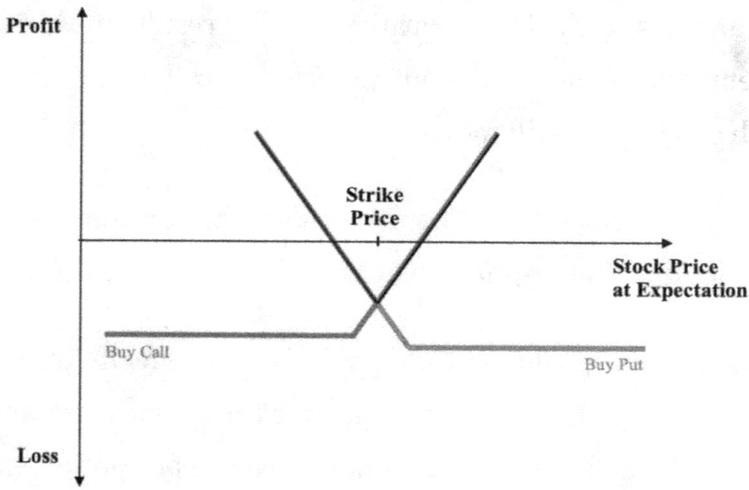

Strategy 2: Iron Condor

An iron condor is one of the most popular options strategies. This is an income-producing strategy, and an iron condor is sold for a net credit (keep this in mind, there is a lot of misinformation about iron condors). An iron condor is sold using a call credit spread, and a put credit spread, all in the same trade. The two options with inner strike prices will be sold. So, for example, suppose that a stock is trading at $200 a share. You could sell a call option with a strike price of $205 and buy a call option with a strike price of $210. Simultaneously, you would sell a put option with a $195 strike price and buy a put option with a $190 strike price.

As long as the stock price stays in between the inner strike prices–ranging between $195 and $205 in our example–you will make a profit. So, we use an iron condor when you expect the stock price will not change very much over the lifetime of the options. All options used in an iron condor have the same expiration date.

To pick your strike prices, determine where support and resistance are. You want to set the strike price of the put option you sell a bit above the support price and set the strike price of the call option you sell a little below the resistance price. Then set the outer strike prices slightly above the resistance price level for the purchased call option and below the support price level for the purchased put option. Many traders make a full-time living strictly selling iron condors. The chart has the following form.

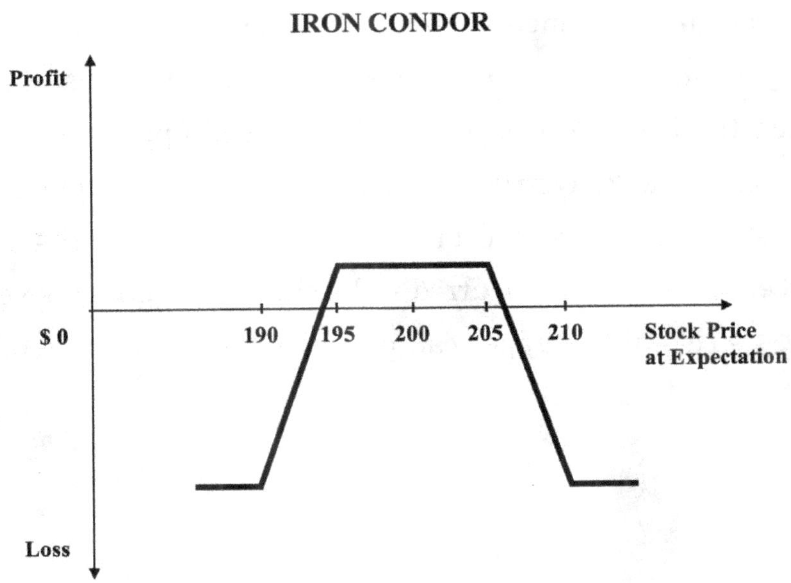

You will receive a net credit for the call credit spread, and a net credit for the put credit spread. The total credit received is your maximum profit. If the stock remains in between the inner strike prices, this is when you will earn profits.

One advantage of the iron condor is that losses are also capped. The maximum loss, should the stock move to the upside, is the difference in strike prices of the two call options. Should the stock move downward, the maximum loss is the difference between the strike prices of the put options. Using our example here would be a $5 loss (per share—total $500) if the stock moved below $190, or above $210.

Strategy 3: Iron Butterfly

An iron butterfly is a less popular way to set this up since it creates a narrow range for the stock. With an iron butterfly, you set your inner strike prices the same. So, for example, using a stock trading at $200, we could sell a call option and a put option with a $200 strike price, and then buy a call option with a $205 strike price, and buy a put option with a $195 strike price. Losses will be incurred if the stock price goes above the $205 strike of the upper call or below the $195 strike of the put.

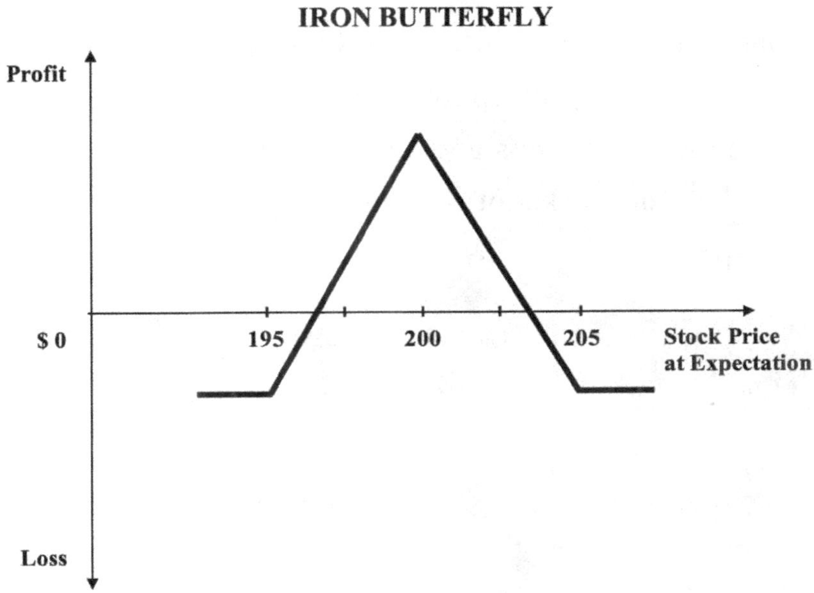

Bonus strategies

Equity Collar

This is a strategy used to hedge risk. It is used on a long stock position that you have, and this is used by large traders. So, to use this strategy, you would have a large number of shares of some stock. If you are uncertain about the direction of the stock that you own, you could set up an equity collar to hedge your risk with put and call options. You set it up by buying an equal number of put and call options with strike prices above the share price for the call options and strike prices below the share price for put options. The options will all have the same expiration date. If the share price moves above the call strike price, you will earn profits on the call options, and the put options will expire worthlessly. If the stock price moves below the put options, the call options will expire worthlessly. You can exercise the put options and sell your stock at a price that is higher than the market price or sell the put options for a profit and keep your stock.

EQUITY COLLAR

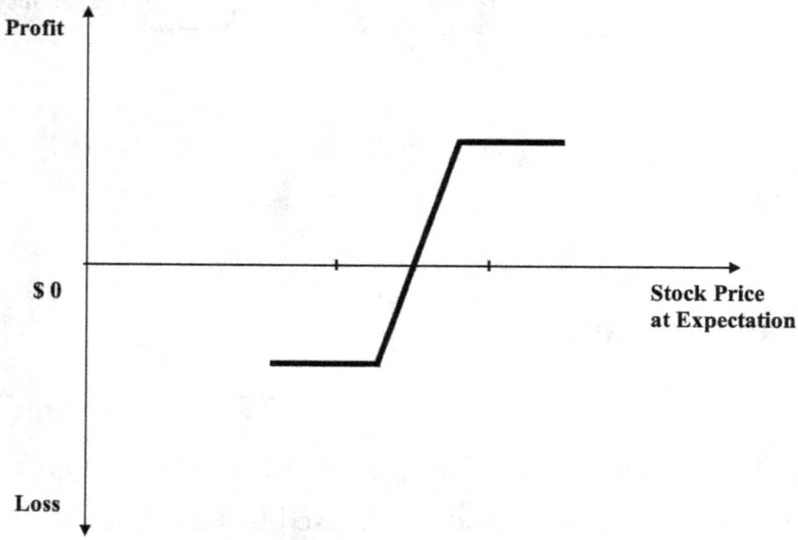

Short Gut

A short gut is a less popular options strategy that involves selling a call and a put option simultaneously. You sell the two options with the same expiration month, but not necessarily the same expiration date. First, you sell a call option at a certain strike price, and then you sell a put option with a higher strike price. Maximum losses are uncapped if the stock price moves in either direction, so you are hoping the stock price will stay the same. Maximum profit is equal to the premiums received from selling the options. This is a little-used strategy and you must be a level 4 options trader to use it, and you must have enough cash in your account to cover selling the two options (cash as collateral).

Long Gut

A long gut involves buying a call option and buying a put option with a higher strike price. Here, you are hoping to make a profit from the stock moving in either direction, so it is someone analogous to a strangle, but you are doing it with the strike prices of the call and put reversed. If the stock price moves up, you will make money from the call but lose money on the put, and if the strike price moves down, you will make money on the put and lose on the call.

Synthetic Strategies

Synthetic strategies are obscure and rarely used by small traders. To make a synthetic put, you must have a large margin account. To set it up, you will short the stock, so you will borrow shares of stock from the broker and sell them on the market, hoping to buy them back at a lower price. Then you will buy a call option on the same stock. If the stock price rises, you will make a profit on the call option to help offset the loss of having to buy the shares back at a higher price (if you borrow shares from the broker, you have to buy them back and return them to the broker at some point). If the stock price drops as expected, you will lose money on the call option which will expire worthlessly, but you will make the expected profit from shorting the stock. You can buy it back at the lower share price, return the shares to the broker, and then the profit from doing that less the cost of the call option is your net profit. So, this involves shorting stock using a call option as insurance.

Chapter 6

Risk Management

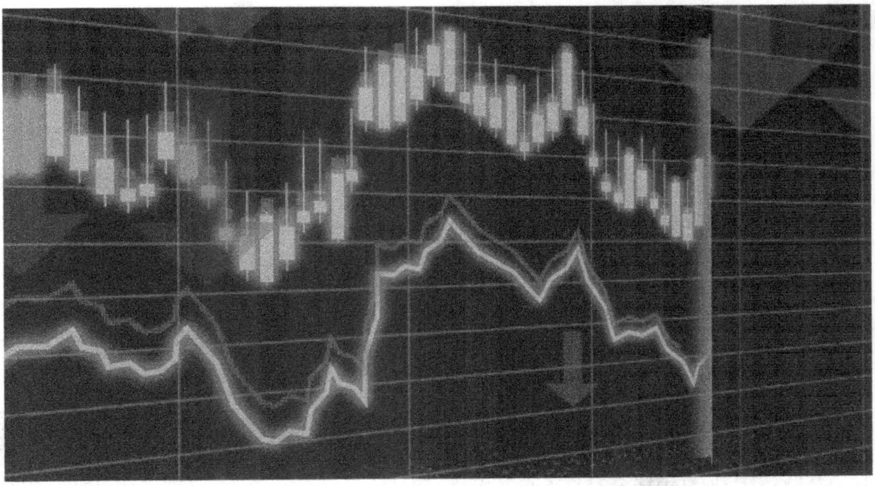

Excellent risk management can save the worst trading strategy, but horrible risk management will sink even the best plan. This is a lesson that many traders learn painfully over time, and I suggest you learn this by heart and install it deep within you even if you can't fully comprehend that statement.

Risk management has many distinct elements to both quantitative and qualitative. With options trading, the quantitative side is minimal thanks to the nature of options limiting risk by themselves. However, the qualitative side deserves a lot of attention.

Risk

So, what is risk anyway? Logically, it is the probability of you losing all of your money. In trading terms, you can think of it as being the probability of your actions, putting you on a path to losing all of your capital. A suitable way to think about the need for good risk management is to ask yourself what a terrible trader would do? Forget trading, what would a bad businessperson do with their capital?

Well, they would spend it on useless stuff that adds nothing to the bottom line. They would also increase expenses, market poorly, not take care of their employees, and be indiscipline regarding their processes. While trading, you don't have employees or marketing needs, so you need not worry about that.

Do you have suppliers and costs? Well, yes, you do. Your supplier is your broker, and you pay fees to execute your trades. That is the cost of access. In directional trading, you have high costs as well because taking losses is a necessary part of trading. With market neutral or non-directional trading, your losses will be minimal, but you should still seek to minimize them.

What about discipline? Do you think you can trade and analyze the market thoroughly if you've just returned home from your job and are tired? If you didn't sleep well last night? Or if you've argued with your spouse or partner? The point I'm making is that the more you behave like a terrible business owner, the more you increase your risk of failure.

Odds and Averages

Trading requires you to think a bit differently about profitability. I spoke about minimizing costs, and your first thought must have been to seek to reduce losses and maximize wins. This is a natural product of linear or ordered thinking. The market, however, is chaotic, and linear thinking will get you nowhere.

Instead, you need to think in terms of averages and odds. Averages imply that you need to worry about your average loss size and your average win size. Seek to decrease the former and increase the latter. Notice that when we talk about averages, we're not talking about reducing the total number of losses. You can reduce the average by either reducing the sum of your losses or by increasing the number of losing trades while keeping the sum of the loss's constant. This is a shift in thinking you must make.

Thinking in this way sets you up to think in terms of odds because in chaotic systems, all you can bank on are odds playing out in the long run. For example, if you flip a coin, do you know in advance whether it will be a head or tail? Probably not. But if someone asked you to predict the distribution of heads versus tails over 10,000 flips, you could guess that it'll be 5000 heads and 5000 tails. You might be off by a few flips either way, but you'll be close percentage-wise.

In fact, the greater the number of flips, the lesser your error percentage. This is because the odds inherent in a pattern that occurs in a chaotic system express themselves best over the long run. Your trading strategy is precisely such a pattern. The market is a chaotic system. Hence, you should focus on executing your strategy as it is meant to be executed repeatedly and worry about profitability only in the long run.

Contrast this with the usual attitude of traders who seek to win every single trade. This is impossible to accomplish since no trading strategy or pattern is correct 100% of the time. If we were discussing directional strategies, I'd spend a lot more time on this, but the fact is that options take care of a lot of this ambiguity themselves.

This is because you don't have to do much when trading options. You enter and then monitor the trade. Sure, it helps to have some directional bias, but even if you get it wrong, your losses will be limited, and you're more likely to hit winners than losers.

Despite this, always think of your strategy in terms of its odds. There are two basic metrics to measure this. The first is the win rate of your system. This is the percentage of winners you have. The second is your payout ratio, which is the average win size divided by the average loss size.

Together these two metrics will determine how profitable your system is. Both of them play off one another, and an increase in one is usually met by a decrease in another. It takes a skillful trader to increase both simultaneously.

Risk Per Trade

The quantitative side of risk management for options trading is lesser than what you need to take care of when trading directionally. However, this doesn't mean there's nothing to worry about. Perhaps the most important metric of them all is your risk per trade. The risk per trade ultimately governs your profitability.

How much should you risk per trade? Common wisdom says that you should restrict this to 2% of your capital. For options trading purposes, this is fine. In fact, once you build your skill and can see opportunities better, I'd suggest increasing it to a higher level.

A point that you must understand here is that you must keep your risk per trade consistent for it to have any effect. You might see a wonderful setup and think it has no chance of failure, but the truth is that you don't know how things will turn out. Even the prettiest setup has every chance of failing, and the ugliest setup you can think of may result in a profit. So never adjust your position size based on how something looks.

Calculating your position size for a trade is a straightforward task. Every option's strategy will have a fixed maximum risk amount. Divide the capital risk by this amount, and that gives you your position size. Round that down to the nearest whole number since you can only buy whole number lots with contract sizes.

For example, let's say your maximum risk is $50 per lot on the trade. Your capital is $10,000. Your risk per trade is 2%. So, the amount you're risking on that trade is 2% of 10,000, which is $200. Divide this by 50, and you get 4. Hence, your position size is four contracts or 400 shares. (You'll buy the contracts, not the shares.)

Why is it important to keep your risk per trade consistent? Well, recall that your average win and lose size is important for determining your profitability. These, with your strategy's success rate, determine how much money you'll make. If you keep shifting your risk amount per trade, you'll shift your win and lose sizes. You might argue that since it's an average, you can always adjust amounts to reflect an average.

My counter to that is, how would you know which trades to adjust in advance? You won't know which ones will be a win or a loss, so you won't know which trade sizes to adjust to meet the average. Hence, keep it consistent across all trades and let the math work for you.

Aside from risk per trade, there are some simple metrics you should keep track of as part of your quantitative risk management plan.

Drawdown

A drawdown refers to the reduction in capital your account experiences. Drawdowns by themselves always occur. The metrics you should measure are the maximum drawdown and recovery period. If you think of your account's balance as a curve, the maximum drawdown is the biggest peak-to-trough distance in dollars. The recovery period is the subsequent time it took for your account to make new equity high.

If your risk per trade is far too high, your max drawdown will be unacceptably high. For example, if you risk 10% per trade and lose two in a row, which is likely, your drawdown will be 20%. This is a gigantic hole to dig your way out. Consider that your capital has decreased by 20%, and the subsequent climb back up needs to be done on lesser capital than previously.

This is why you need to keep your risk per trade low and in line with your strategy's success rate. The best way to manage drawdowns and limit the damage they cause is to put in place risk limits per day, week, and month. Even professional athletes who train to do one thing all the time have awful days, so it's unfair to expect yourself to be at 100% all the time.

These risk limits will take you out of the game when you're playing poorly. A daily risk limit is to prevent you from getting into a spiral of revenge trading. A good limit to stick to when starting off is to stop trading if you experience three losses in a row. This is unlikely with options trades to be honest unless you screw up badly, but it's good to have a limit in place from a perspective of discipline.

Next, aim for a maximum weekly drawdown limit of 5% and a monthly drawdown limit of 6-8%. These are high limits, to be honest, and if you are a directional trader, these limits do not apply to you. Directional traders need to be a lot more conservative than options trader with risk.

Understand that these are hard stop limits. So, if your account has hit its monthly drawdown level within the first week, you need to take the rest of the month off. Over-trading and a lack of reflection on progress can cause a lot of damage, and a drawdown is a reflection of that.

Qualitative Risk

Quantitative metrics aside, your ability to properly manage qualitative things in your life and trading will dictate a lot of your success. Prepare well, and you're likely to see progress. You need to see preparation as your responsibility. I mean, no one else can prepare for you, can they?

There are different elements to tracking your level of preparation, so let's look at them one by one.

Health

You can't trade if you're physically unfit. If you have a fever or if you're suffering from some condition that makes it impossible for you to concentrate, forget about trading. You can be rest assured that the other traders in the market will be more than happy to take your money.

When viewed from an options trading perspective, the risk is even more acute. All options strategies will require you to write options at some point, even the most basic ones like in this book. Even if your position is covered, making a mistake, and having an option you wrote to be exercised by the buyer is an unpleasant thing that happens. Maintain a regimen of exercise and eat healthy food. Depending on how long you sit in front of your screen, you might even want to consider avoiding certain foods when in session.

Heavy meals and food that makes you drowsy will cause your performance to dip, so avoid eating them when you're in the market. Also, don't exercise to such an extent that you're completely exhausted. The idea is to be fresh and alert, not fatigued and aching for a good sleep.

You might have an image of traders as being highly wired and as people who spend their entire lives in front of a screen. Well, most traders sit in front of a screen most of the time, but the successful ones make time for other stuff in their lives. So, don't copy some false vision here. Instead, do what feels comfortable to you while taking care to not slip into habits that are detrimental to your success.

Lifestyle

Your fitness is just one part of your lifestyle. Is your lifestyle conducive to profitable trading? Are you someone who loves staying up during odd hours and considers it normal to stumble onto a work task while hungover or worse? Make no mistake, the market will make you donate all of your capital to it.

Many beginners underestimate how difficult trading is. This should come as no surprise since beginners, by definition, underestimate anything. What shocks most of them is the degree to which they underestimate the difficulty of trading successfully. Let me put it in writing for you: Trading is one of the most challenging things you will ever do in your life.

The reason it is so difficult is that of the ever-changing nature of the market and the mental demands it places upon you. Another key lifestyle question to consider is the hours when you'll trade. Most of you reading this probably have full-time jobs and cannot spend your whole day in front of the market.

So, plan out when you'll trade and how you'll prepare yourself for the session. What routines will you carry out? If you will trade in the morning before work begins, how will you manage to do this? Will you work in a quiet place or in some noisy truck stop on the way to work? Options positions don't need a lot of maintenance, so there's not much need for this, but when will you check in on the market throughout the day? Will you check in a few times? Five times? Define everything to do with your routine.

Think of yourself as a professional athlete who has to show up for a game every day. An athlete has a precise method of preparation before showing up for a game. They don't deviate from their preparatory routine and don't experiment with new things during game time. Practice is when they try out fresh stuff.

How will you practice your skills and improve your ability to execute your strategy? When will you do this? Plan it all out and develop your success routine.

Mental States

Trading is a mental activity. You need not lift or push anything physically. Therefore, it is crucial to ensure that your mental state is as optimal as it needs to be for you to execute correctly. Having a checklist or a mental check-in list works wonders for the trading process.

Before any trading, write what's going through your mind and ask yourself how you feel. If you find that you're tired or frustrated and unable to focus properly, step away, and do not trade. If you're planning on sitting in front of your terminal for more than an hour, make it a habit to check in with yourself every half hour or hourly. This need not be a detailed examination, just a simple check-in with yourself to see how things are going.

Take your risk management tasks seriously, and the market will reward you with profits. Do not be the trader who stumbles into the market completely unprepared and then wonders why trading is so unforgiving. Above all else, seek to eliminate all sources of stress when it comes to trading. Take regular breaks and schedule months off from the market to recap and assimilate the things you've learned and need to improve.

Trading every single day of the year does not make sense. This isn't a job where you'll be rewarded with a guaranteed salary for just showing up. You need to produce results, and to do so, you need to manage your downside carefully.

An excellent practice is to actually review how you work and set aside months only for trading and months exclusively for practice. By practice, I mean examining your prior results, working on your mindset, and improving your risk management abilities. This is an unconventional method of working, but it will pay massive dividends down the line.

Now that you have a better understanding of the basics, it's finally time to jump in and look at various trading strategies you can deploy with options.

Chapter 7

Call vs Put Options Trading

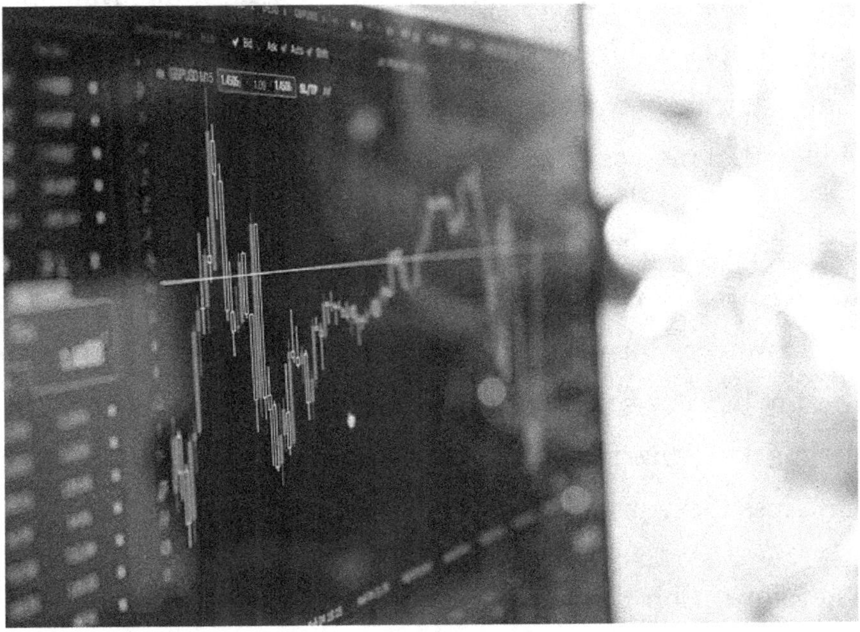

In this field of text, we will discuss the difference between call option and put option.

Jacob's Call Option Trade

Jacob is a farmer, and a cattle breeder who owns several dairy cows. Bob, who is an acquaintance of Jacob, is a trader of farm animals.

One day Bob gets a tip from a friend that the town's main dairy was negotiating a deal with a big international chocolate manufacturing company. If the deal were to materialize, the chocolate company would triple the quantity of milk they purchase from the dairy every day. To meet this increase in demand, the dairy would also have to increase milk production, and for increasing production, they would have to purchase many dairy cows at short notice. This move could result in a substantial increase in cow prices locally.

Bob realized he could make some excellent profits if he bought some cows from Jacob and then sold them after the prices went up. However, Bob wasn't entirely sure about this tip and did not want to buy cows upfront at the full price of $2,000 (which was the market price for a dairy cow at that time) and later sell out for a loss if the price did not rise as expected.

Therefore, Bob approaches Jacob and makes him a unique offer.

Bob tells Jacob that he will pay the latter a sum of $50 upfront for the right to buy one of his cows at the prevailing market price of $2,000, for the next 30 days. Also, Jacob would be under no obligation to return that amount if Bob no longer wanted to exercise his right (if cow prices dropped below $2,000).

Jacob saw no reason for cow prices rising anytime soon and was therefore glad to sign a contract to receive $50 from trader Bob in exchange for giving Bob the right to buy a cow at $2,000 for the next 30 days.

However, Jacob puts forth a condition that the proposed contract should cover 5 cows and not just 1 cow, and that meant Bob would have to pay $250 for the right to purchase 5 cows for a 30-day period.

Bob agrees to Jacob's condition, and therefore, Jacob pockets Bob's $250 and then signs the contract - the contract that gave Bob the right (but not the obligation) to buy 5 of Jacob's cows at the price of $2,000 for the next 30 days.

Bob knew that in the next 30 days, the market price of cows would either rise (as per his expectations), or continue to stay the same, or perhaps even fall (in the worst-case scenario).

If the market price for cows stayed the same at $2,000 or fell below that value in the next 30 days, Bob would have to give up the $250 he paid Jacob to get the agreement in place. Bob was under no obligation to buy cows at a lower price, and hence his losses will be curtailed to $250 only–the money he paid Jacob to sign the contract.

On the other hand, if the market price for cows went up within the next 30 days, Bob would approach Jacob to get 5 cows at

$2,000 each and Jacob would be contractually obliged to sell the cows at $2,000, irrespective of how much more the cows were worth at that time.

Bob waits.

Three weeks after they put the contract in place, the town dairy signed a deal with the chocolate company to increase their daily supply of milk to the chocolate company by almost 4 times. To meet that demand, the dairy started purchasing many dairy cows at increasingly higher rates that resulted in the prices of dairy cows surging by almost 25% in the locality.

Following this price surge, Bob goes to Jacob and exercises his right to buy the 5 cows at $2,000 each. Bob then goes ahead and sells these cows to the dairy at $2,500 each.

Bob, thereby, makes a total profit of $2,250 for these 5 cows ($500 times 5 less the $250 for the contract amount he paid Jacob).

The trade that took place between Bob and Jacob represents how options trade works and if we apply stock market terms into the afore-mentioned scenario then:

A single cow represents one particular underlying Share/Stock. Bob is the Buyer of the contract, and Jacob is the Seller. Since this contract gives the buyer the right to buy–this contract is a Call Option.

$2,000 represents the Market Price of the share of the company (at the time they put the agreement in place).

$2,000 also represents the Strike-Price (SP) or the pre-determined price at which the proposed trade would take place between the buyer (Bob) and the seller (Jacob)–remember that Jacob paid $50 to purchase a cow at a fixed price of $2,000.

The $50 paid against each cow is called the Premium.

The number 5 shows the Lot Size of the contract–it is the fixed number of shares that an individual options contract covers.

Lastly, the 30 days in this scenario denotes the Time to Expiry of the options contract.

I hope you have entirely understood how a call option works now.

Jacob's Put Option Trade

After being forced to sell 5 of his cows at a price lesser than the market price because of his contractual obligation, a slightly disappointed Jacob starts thinking.

From his experience, Jacob has seen that in situations where livestock prices increase sharply due to some change in the environment, the prices eventually come down marginally before reaching stability.

However, Jacob wasn't confident if cow prices had hit the ceiling yet–if he sold off his cows right away and prices continued to rise, he would miss a chance for selling at even better prices. The market price for a cow was $2,500, and Jacob wanted to wait for two weeks and see if it went up any further. If the prices were already at a high and if they dropped sharply, Jacob wanted to ensure that he could sell a few cows for at least $2,400.

Considering his predicament, Jacob gets into a contract similar to the one he had earlier signed with Bob. However, this time, he would be the 'buyer' of the right–the right to sell cows at a fixed price (unlike the right to buy that Bob purchased from him).

For this purpose, Jacob approaches Chad, a livestock trader in the local market, and offers him a deal. The deal was that, for the next 60 days, Jacob would have a right to sell Chad 10 cows at $2,400 each. And to own that right, Jacob would pay $30 per cow - a total of $300 for 10 cows.

Chad agrees and signs up for the deal and pockets the $300 since he didn't expect prices to fall from $2,500, let alone fall below $2,400. As long as cow prices stayed above $2,400 for the next 2 months (which Chad thought was very likely), he had nothing to lose.

A month and a half later, Jacob's prediction turned out to be right, and cow prices dropped to $2,250.

Therefore, Jacob goes to Chad and exercises his right to sell the cows at $2,400.

Since Chad was contractually obliged to buy the cows at $2,400, he has no choice but to buy the cows at the fixed price despite the cows being worth $150 less in the market. Jacob, thereby profits by $1200 ($150 x 10 less than the $300 paid for the contract) off his trade.

Like we did last time, let's apply the various stock market terms to this trade too:

A single cow represents one particular underlying Share/Stock.

Jacob is the Buyer of the contract while Chad is the Seller. Since this contract gives the buyer the right to sell–this contract is a Put Option.

$2,500 - the price of the cow, represents the Market Price of a share (at the time they put the agreement in place).

$2,400 represents the Strike-Price (SP) or the pre-determined price at which the proposed trade would take place between the Buyer (Jacob) and the Seller (Chad).

The $30 paid against each cow is the Premium.

The number 10 indicates the Lot Size of the contract.

Lastly, the 60 days in this scenario denotes the Time to Expiry of the options contract.

If you aren't still completely clear on the difference between call options and put options and all the various terms we have used so far. You want to go through these two examples one more time because you need to be completely thorough with your understanding of these trades to understand the strategies that will be taught.

Chapter 8

Small Account Options Strategies

If you were first to open your contract by selling, we say that you are "short." If you buy to open a position, we say that you are "long." The simplest way to trade options is to take a long position on a call or a put. Although when buying and selling stocks we say that someone "shorts" the stock when they are hoping to profit off a decline in share price, you can expect to profit from a decline in share price, but you are "long" regarding the put option.

The strategy for profiting from going long on a call, or put option is simple. You are hoping the price of the stock would move in your favor so you will earn a profit. The industry is full of naysayers that downplay this basic strategy; however, the reality is you can earn profits in this way. That is buying or selling individual options, be they the call or put variety. **The key to success when doing this type of trading is to stay on top of it and don't buy options on a whim.** You need a good reason to buy a call or a put option by itself, and that means paying attention to the financial news surrounding the company, earnings reports, and looking at simple market trends to determine when you have a reasonable probability of earning a profit.

Before venturing into options trading, it is vital to have a plan of action. Options trading has of late become very popular since it gives individuals a chance to make money fast. This does not mean that no losses occur, but one can also lose enormous amounts of money fast. Options trading strategies range from simple to complex ones with a variety of odd names and payoffs

Long Straddle Strategy

This options strategy is where an option trader purchases both long put and long call for the same asset having a similar strike price and expiration date. This strategy entails enjoying unpredictable and big moves. This strategy is said to be complex due to the sophisticated calculations that are done by options traders. This strategy aims at making profits from any outcome but also has challenges just like any other investment. Risks associated with this strategy is that the market might not react to the event generated by it strongly enough. This, therefore, makes this strategy expensive since it entails investing in two approaches.

This strategy can alternatively be used in capturing the expected increase in the trade's volatility. Implied volatility is very influential when determining the prices of options. An increase in the volatility, therefore, means that there is an increase in all options' prices. Limited risks and unlimited profits characterize this strategy. In case the prices of the stock increase continually, then the advantages expected are limited. On the other hand, if the prices of the stock become zero, then the profit is the difference between the strike price and the premiums that were paid for the purchased options.

Buy-Write Strategy

This strategy is also referred to as the covered call strategy. This strategy is majorly used in stocks. An example of this strategy is the sales of covered calls. This strategy entails the purchase of stocks, and then the investor sells the stock's call options. The primary purpose of this strategy is to generate income from the premiums paid for options. This strategy works by making assumptions that the security's market price would change and might rise before its expiration day. On the other hand, if the option's price declines, the investor would then write a call to keep premiums from the sale of options. This strategy may be used to increase returns by periodically repeating it when the time for the options is lackluster.

To implement this strategy accurately, the option's strike price should always be higher than compared to the price of the stock. This, therefore, needs well-executed judgment as the strike price should be higher but not as making the premium price insignificant. If the expiration period is set to be prolonged, then this means that the premiums will also be high. This strategy might lose its position in case the price of options rises rapidly.

Married Put Strategy

This strategy is also referred to as a synthetic long call. Married put strategy is an options trading strategy that entails the trader purchasing put options together with shares equivalent to the purchased stock. We use this strategy is common in cases where the investor acts bullish on certain stocks and might want to benefit from the stock. Its profit potential is unlimited and is like that of the long call. This strategy also has got a limited risk, which is usually calculated by the addition of the premium paid to the commissions paid. The break-even point of this strategy is achieved by determining the underlying price. The break-even point is determined by adding the premium paid to the price of underlying securities. This strategy works similarly as an insurance cover having certain strike-price and is against the short-term losses. At the same time frame, the options trader would the very call options at an increased strike price.

Protective Collar Strategy

This strategy is where an options trader purchase shares of an option then sell a short call option and simultaneously purchases a long put to limit downside risks. This strategy majorly aims at protecting stocks that have got a low market price. Protective collar strategy uses call options upon its sale and puts options upon purchase. Here, both put options and call options should have a similar number of shares and expiration date.

This strategy entails the integration of short call, long put options, and long stocks. In options trading, a long stock refers to where a trader purchased underlying assets hoping to earn from them in the future. When using this strategy, it is advisable to take a long-put option if the market price might continuously fall, and you want to prevent further loss of money and limit risks.

An advantage of this strategy is that it is cheap as compared to the purchase of protective put in instances where you will have to sell out your money from your shares. This strategy might be disadvantageous since it limits the profits in instances where the price of stock increases. The protective collar strategy works well with protecting profits got from stock.

Long Strangle Strategy

This strategy is neutral, and it entails simultaneously purchasing an out-of-the-money call, and out-of-the-money put having a similar expiration date and the underlying stock. This strategy is characterized by limited risks and unlimited profits gained from the stocks. This is obtained where the options trader believes that the stock would experience significant volatility. This strategy is a debit spread since debit is usually taken so that one can enter this trade. The large profits for this strategy are usually obtained in cases where the price of an underlying stock fluctuates at expiration day. The maximum loss for this strategy is obtained by adding the total premiums paid to the commissions paid.

Chapter 9

How to Trade Options on Robinhood for Beginners in 2020

What is Robinhood?

To put it simply, Robinhood is an online stock brokerage app for your smartphone. Robinhood differs from other stock trading apps like E*TRADE or TDAmeritrade. The major difference is that instead of charging 5-10 dollars commission on every trade plus additional fees, Robinhood lets you make all your trades for free. They never charge you any commissions or fees, ever. This one simple difference opens up a lot of options for everyday people that were previously only available to the rich. Robinhood even gives away free shares of stocks like Apple, Microsoft, Ford, Sirius XM radio just for downloading their app.

When and Why to use Robinhood

Robinhood is still a new company. Using their app, you don't get the benefits of having your stocks in an IRA or Roth IRA. I wouldn't suggest using it to hold your life savings. What Robinhood is good for is starting a stock portfolio from nothing and building it with as little cost as possible to sizeable amounts, then transfer to an IRA or Roth IRA for long-term benefits. In our series, we will be using Robinhood to make more short-term trades with the goal of maximizing growth in less than 5 years.

Downloading the app and getting your first free share of stock

Robinhood will give you a free share of stock just for downloading the app and opening an account. The accounts are free to open, so it won't cost you anything to open one. All you have to do is download the app using a referral link like this one CLICK HERE TO DOWNLOAD THE ROBINHOOD APP AND GET YOUR FIRST FREE STOCK. Enter your name and information to open an account. Then look under the menu select Free Stocks. On this page, you will see a link in the top right corner saying PAST INVITES click on this link to claim your free stock. You can also see a list of all the free stocks you receive here. Robinhood will give you 1 free share of a stock drawn at random from their inventory for every person you refer to using their app.

Watchlist and Search functions

Robinhood has a watch list just like any other stock trading platform allowing you to track the price movements of your favorite stocks. It comes preloaded with some of the most popular stocks like Facebook, Apple, Google, and Amazon. While you can trade these stocks on Robinhood, They are rather expensive anywhere from $100 to $1000. We will focus on using the search function to find stocks that are more affordable for beginners and adding them to our watch list. Robinhood does not suggest stocks for you to buy, and they don't have a list of all the stocks available. So, as far as finding stocks that you want to buy, you're pretty much on your own. You can search for stock tips and things like that on Google to find companies likely to go up in price and get the symbols for those companies like Facebook is FB, and Apple is AAPL. Once you see the symbol for a company that you like to go to the Robinhood app and click on the little magnifying glass in the top right corner. Type in the symbol you found, and you will see the company come up. From here, you will see a little circle with a plus symbol inside. You can click on this symbol to add a company to your watch list. Or, you can click on the name of the company for more details about the stock like price, volume, avg volume, market cap, dividend ratios, and so forth.

Buying your first stock

By now I'm sure you're ready to get started buying and selling the stock for a profit. I suggest you start small and work your way up. Find a stock you can afford and add it to your watch list. On your watch list, click on the stock you want to buy, and the details page will come up. At the bottom of the page, there is a button that will say trade or buy. Click on this button to start the buy order. Robinhood will automatically bring up the form to place a market order. Type in how many shares you want to buy and click send. You need to know that when using a market order, Robinhood may purchase the stock at up to a 5% higher price than the current market price. To buy stocks at a specific price, you need to use a limit order. You can change the order type by clicking on the link in the top right corner of the trading screen

Market and Limit orders what are they used for

Basically, market orders tell Robinhood that you want to vend this stock at whatever the market price is regardless of if it goes up or down. If you put in an order to buy shares, Robinhood will automatically purchase available shares at up to 5% over the current market price. Anything more than 5%, and it will not complete the order. Or, if you place an order to sell, it will sell at whatever the current market price is even if it drops rapidly.

A limit order tells Robinhood that you want to vend this stock but only if it is available at a specific price. If you use the link in the top right corner of the trading screen to change the order type to a limit order, Robinhood will prompt you to enter the exact price you are about to pay for that stock, and it will only complete the order if it is available at the price you enter or lower. Or if you're selling, you will be prompted to enter the minimum amount your willing to vend for, and it will only be completed when the price reaches that point or greater.

Stop-loss and stop-limit orders what are they used for

A stop-loss order is an order to vend a stock if it reaches a specific price point. This type of order is your safety net, and we will be using it a lot later in our series to minimize risk. If you switch your order type to this, it will prompt you to enter a price. If you are buying, you want to enter the price you want to buy at and when the stock reaches that price, or higher your order will be converted to an order. If you are selling you, want to enter a price so that if the price of the stock falls below that point, your order will be converted to an order. This is useful because it allows you to set up a safety net, so you don't have to be watching your stocks constantly to avoid a loss. For example, you buy a stock for $5.00. You set your stop loss in order to sell if the price falls below $4.95. If the price goes up, you will continue to hold the stock and make money. If the price drops below $4.95, your order will convert to order and sell the stock to avoid further losses.

A stop-limit order is an order to vend a stock at a specific price point. But will convert to a limit order when the stock hits that point. You must set two price points for a stop-limit order. One price point at which to convert the order and another at which to limit an order. What this allows you to do is to create in which to buy the stock. For example, you think if a certain stock breaks past its 52-week high, it will get a bump from lots of people hoping it will continue to go up. But once that initial wave of buyers is over, the volume will go back to normal, and it will go back down some then continue to rise slowly. Let's say the stock is $8 per share. The 52-week high is $10 per share. You place a stop-limit order with the converted price at $10 per share and the limit at $15 per share. A large hedge fund buys into the stock and places a large order for millions of shares at the end of the day. The stock skyrockets to $20 in after-hours trading. You're using a free account, so your orders can't execute after-market hours. In the morning, when the markets open, the big players have already completed their orders. The price is still $20 but drops because no small investors are willing to pay such a hefty price. Had you used a stop-loss order, you would have purchased the stock at an exorbitant price, and then it would fall back down. But by using a stop-limit order you won't buy any shares unless the price is below $15.

Leave a 1-Click Review!

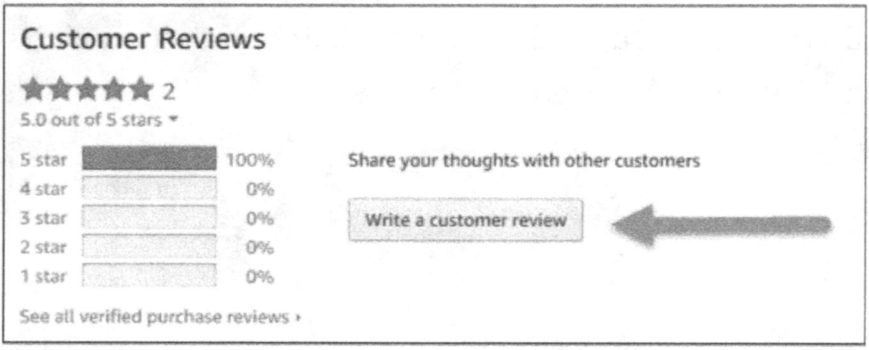

I would be incredibly thankful if you could take just 60 seconds to write a brief review on Amazon, even if it's just a few sentences!

Scan the QR code or follow the link below to leave a quick review

SCAN ME

https://www.amazon.com/review/create-review?asin=B088QNMTV8

Conclusion

You are at the end of the book, and I would like to thank you for reading through it and making it to the end. Let's be hopeful it has been helpful enough to provide the knowledge and skills that are needed to trade in options as a newbie in the market. And as not everything might have been covered in this book outline, it would also be great if you would seek to enrich yourself with such knowledge from other sources apart from this book. The book has nonetheless covered great subjects on introducing the options market to a new and a beginner trader that seeks to apprentice the reader to the market. Written in this outline, as you've read, is a comprehensive guide to starting trading in options.

As the primary subject of the book is, we have discussed the rudiments of options trading, offering the reader a clear picture of what options reading is. We also encourage you to start on trading options by the book, outlining the advantages of the trade that leaves you motivated to start on it already. We make you aware of the fundamentals of the trade and the components of it, further expanding your knowledge of the options market, which will prove very helpful to a beginner in the market, for they are well aware of what options trading comprises.

The highlight of the book to the reader is talking about how to get started in trading the options. This part offers you the practical skills and gears you up to take the first step in making your beginner trade. The knowledge written in this book would be to zero if you, the reader, who is a beginner trader, would not make the first trade, following care guidelines. And this book has just done that. Written great and helpful tactics to kick you off as you start your journey in the options trading world. After gaining such skills, use them in the real market world and get to experience the highs and the lows, but as stated in the book, nonetheless brilliant strategies.

As a beginner in trading, you have also benefited from other aspects written in the book, such as risk and risk management, very crucial leverage, and others such as technical analysis. These aspects will be vital in trading, for in most cases, that determine the profitability of the trades you have made. Let's hope that you have gone through these aspects painstakingly and taken away the key points that will be crucial when you are trading. Factors such as leverage will distinguish you from becoming a professional trader in no time and a trader who makes mistakes and errors that would have otherwise been avoided. We have discussed extensively technical analysis in the book as one of the critical issues to dwell on when you begin to trade.

As observed in the book, we can term it as the backbone that holds the trading. It is the most important takeaway you can take. Without the analysis, your takeoff as a beginner trader would be baseless, for you would make assumptions on the market with no reference, which is a suicidal thing to do in the market. It is of great importance to traders in this book outline as they progress from being beginners is the subject of psychology in trading. We are hopeful that you will learn from this outline the importance of trading with your emotions kept in check, as the book advertises, for successful trading. Apply this knowledge in real-time trading and approach the market in the right mental state, this being one of the skills that were mentioned in the psychology of options trading.

As a beginner, probably the most exciting part of the book was where tips on succeeding in options trading were extensively written. This should buoy your beginner trading spirits up and gear you up for being successful in this field, which you'll be, after following the tips outlined here and from many other sources. To be fully confident in your trading capacities and abilities, this outline had also provided in text form of the mistakes that are to be avoided when you are trading.

All this said, it remains up to you, the beginner reader of trading in options to make the most crucial move; and that is making your first trade. This should not be procrastinated as the book has prepared you enough for the market, and you should be confident to make trades, and also make it a learning experience from your gains and losses, which are a sure thing to make in trading. Also, be sure to get useful information from enlightening sources to keep you on top-notch. We hope the skills that you've gathered from this exceptional book will prove helpful as you trade and make your way in options trading. We wish you the best of luck as you start on this enthralling endeavor in your life, packed with all the information you need. May you make the best trades and predictions with this outline as your guiding ray.

Thank you for taking the time to go through this outline, and if you found the contents of this book to be helpful, please do a review of it on any platform, which we will appreciate.

The Options Trading Checklist

(<u>Good Luck</u> Trading Without this...)

This checklist includes:

- ❑ 5 Option Strategies that Every Trader Should Know About!
- ❑ 5 Stocks to Buy in the 2020 Stock Market Crash
- ❑ The Top 3 Options Trading Strategies for Beginners
- ❑ The 5 Secrets of Getting Rich (Bonus)

To receive your survival checklist, visit the link below:

https://davidjohnson.activehosted.com/f/9

CPSIA information can be obtained
at www.ICGtesting.com
Printed in the USA
LVHW090847101220
672446LV00035B/48

9 781801 208062